The Almighty & the Dollar

The Almighty & the Dollar

A Lifestyle of Generosity

BRIAN COCHRAN
& JOHN MOORE

john moore
associates

The Almighty & the Dollar: A Lifestyle of Generosity
By Brian Cochran and John Moore

Edited by Adam Colwell's WriteWorks, LLC: Adam Colwell and Ginger Colwell
Cover concept and marketing consultation: McKee Wallwork & Company
Cover designer: Jimmy Anaya
Interior design and typesetting: Katherine Lloyd, The DESK
Published by Author2Market/D&L Press: Brad Smith

Printed in the United States of America

ISBN (Paperback): 978-1-7339956-6-5
ISBN (eBook): 978-1-7339956-7-2

The information contained in this book does not purport to be a complete description of the securities, markets, or developments referred to in this material. The information has been obtained from sources considered to be reliable, but we do not guarantee that the foregoing material is accurate or complete. Any information is not a complete summary or statement of all available data necessary for making an investment decision and does not constitute a recommendation. Investing involves risk and you may incur a profit or loss regardless of strategy selected, including diversification and asset allocation.

Any opinions provided are those of the authors (John Moore and Brian Cochran), Ron Blue, or any other individuals listed in the book. Expressions of opinion are as of the initial book publishing date and are subject to change without notice. All financial, retirement and estate planning should be individualized as each person's situation is unique. This information is not intended as a solicitation or an offer to buy or sell any security referred to herein. Keep in mind that there is no assurance that our recommendations or strategies will ultimately be successful or profitable nor protect against a loss. There may also be the potential for missed growth opportunities that may occur after the sale of an investment. Recommendations, specific investments or strategies discussed may not be suitable for all investors. Past performance may not be indicative of future results. You should discuss any tax or legal matters with the appropriate professional.

Any case studies presented are for illustrative purposes only. Individual cases will vary. Prior to making any investment decision, you should consult with your financial advisor about your individual situation.

Contents

Acknowledgements

We have drawn from much wisdom, and called upon many helpful hands, in the creation of this book. The insights from Kingdom Advisors and Generous Giving have informed and inspired the content, and we are grateful for their contributions.

Some of the content was drawn from a book originally titled and released as *The Almighty and the Dollar*, by Family Life Communications, Inc. in 1998. This book was edited by Adam and Ginger Colwell of Adam Colwell's WriteWorks thanks to a timely recommendation from Rod Robison. We are thankful for their superb work and Rod's excellent referral.

We are also indebted to McKee Wallwork & Company for encouraging us to revisit John's original material from 1998 and write this book on financial principles. John had already written the original *The Almighty and the Dollar* when his introduction to Ron Blue's teachings during a three-day, in-person seminar changed how he viewed finances and giving. Sitting under Ron's teaching caused John to realize how much more he can do to be even more effective and go deeper with his clients.

Finally, we are thankful for Rob West's leadership in Kingdom Advisors, and his MoneyWise Radio program is invaluable in bringing quality information about the principles of finance to the public.

Meet the Authors

Brian Cochran has been part of the JMA team since 2013. As a CERTIFIED FINANCIAL PLANNER™ professional and a Certified Kingdom Advisor, Brian collaborates with tax advisors, attorneys, and insurance professionals to help meet the financial objectives of the families he serves. Brian's desire is to convey the principles that make people successful with their finances in a simple way and get rid of the intimidation and fear surrounding money management. He sees *Almighty & the Dollar: A Lifestyle of Generosity* as an opportunity to help more people experience contentment, joy, and confidence about finances. Brian is a sports enthusiast and spends his free time watching, playing, and coaching basketball. He especially enjoys traveling to see Portland Trailblazer games with his wife, Emily, and their two sons.

John Moore founded John Moore Associates (JMA) in 1997 with a passion to help people reach a point of contentment with what God has given them so they are freed up to be more generous in many ways, not just financially. A Certified Kingdom Advisor, John's life verse from the Bible is 1 Timothy 6:6: "Godliness with contentment is great gain." His diligent stewardship is in part refined by his military experience, which instilled in him a strong sense of discipline and strategic thinking. John now uses these skills to develop and refine optimal strategies tailored to the needs of each family he advises. An avid pilot, John enjoys flying both airplanes and gliders and spending time with his wife of over 40 years, Connie.

Introducing the Lifestyle

The United States has never before had more wealth than it does right now. Because we live in such an affluent society, we have a responsibility to be held accountable for our financial decisions. Even more, we have a duty to ourselves and those around us to be generous with our money—and generosity is what *The Almighty & the Dollar: A Lifestyle of Generosity* is all about.

Amazingly, a recent poll said that 41 percent of Americans with annual incomes of $200,000 or more complain, and even feel depressed, because they believe they don't have enough money. That same article indicated that Millennials who use automated bank payments are 40 percent more likely to overdraw their accounts, showing our tendency to mismanage the abundance we have.[1] In addition, an Albuquerque, NM area foundation did a study on giving based on metropolitan statistical areas around the country. Its findings showed that lower income individuals actually give more as a percentage of income than people in higher income brackets.[2]

Yet our anxiety about, and misuse of, our money can be lessened and even eliminated as we begin practicing the principles shared in *The Almighty & the Dollar: A Lifestyle of Generosity*. These principles of financial responsibility and giving are not complex. They're quite simple, but that doesn't mean they are going to be easy to implement because they tug against our nature and our desires. Giving more is hard because we want to have more, keep more, and feel we need more.

In general, people tend to be either givers, spenders, or savers. The spenders will spend the greater income. The savers will save more out of fear of what the future might hold or out of greed. Both share the prevailing attitude that they will give when they have more, but they never feel like they actually do have more. They never think they have enough to give, even if their income is twice what it was 15 years ago. They adopt the attitude that they will give later when they are rich. "If I win the lottery," they say, "then I will give a lot of it away."

But you don't have to wait to win the lottery to be generous. It's not the dollar amount you give that matters, but the proportion that you give from what you already have. We've met someone who intentionally gives away 55 percent of her income. When asked why, she declared, "I only deduct 50 percent. That's the tax rule, and if I am not giving some extra that I can't write off on my taxes, I'm not sure my heart is in the right place." Then she rubbed her hands together and laughed. "It drives my accountant crazy."

The Almighty & the Dollar: A Lifestyle of Generosity will also provide the wisdom behind the principles we share so that you will understand why it is good and beneficial to be generous. You'll find references to biblical principles throughout the book. The reason we use the Bible as a resource is because there are over 2,000 wisdom-filled references to money within its pages. If you are a believer in God, think of this as God's Word speaking into your day-to-day finances. If you are not a believer, just know that this timeless wisdom has been experienced or tested over thousands of years to help with your financial decisions. This knowledge will better motivate you to be disciplined and execute principles such as saving or debt elimination. In addition, portions of the book address couples specifically, but anyone from singles to widows will find the concepts and insights shared to be helpful and an encouragement to properly handle your finances and develop a lifestyle of generous giving.

Finally, *The Almighty & the Dollar: A Lifestyle of Generosity* will help you discover that generosity is born out of contentment and gratitude. If you don't *feel* like you have enough and are not thankful for what you already have, it is going to be really difficult to give because you are first going to take care of what you think you need. Another obstacle to contentment and gratitude we face as Americans is that we are fiercely independent and want to be in control. Releasing control of our finances is counterculture, counterintuitive, and uncomfortable. But once you give up that control, you will discover that contentment itself has incredible value, as 1 Timothy 6:6 says: "Yet true godliness with contentment is itself great wealth."

It's not surprising that studies have shown that people are the happiest when they are giving their money away.[3] The other interesting thing as shown by a Harris survey from 2018 is that people really enjoy receiving gifts of experiences rather than stuff.[4]

Our materialistic culture screams, "Buy more! Buy more!" yet the more content, fulfilling path is to, "Give more! Give more!"

The Almighty & the Dollar: A Lifestyle of Generosity offers you an amazing opportunity to take the principles we'll share, put them into practice, and unleash a way of living that aims to make you joyful, thankful, and content with where you are financially, who you are individually, and where you are going.

Let's get started!

1

You're the Manager,
Not the Owner

Before we dive into the principles that impact your decisions on finances, we need to first determine your attitude about money—because having the correct mindset will go a long way in determining your actions.

One of our youngest team members at John Moore Associates possessed the ideal perspective of what it meant to be a manager, not an owner. How?

Sometimes, he needed to drive not just a company car, but John's personal car. When he was behind the wheel, he drove that car far more carefully than he did his own vehicle. Why was that? Because he was a steward of the boss's car. He didn't own it, but he knew he was managing it and had to do it well.

We then joked with him, "That's a good thing. Your car seems to have more scratches than ours."

All kidding aside, he got it. When taking John's car somewhere for an errand, he was fully in control of the vehicle. He could do with it whatever he wanted, and John couldn't stop him. But the young man released his control by realizing whose car he was driving. It wasn't his, so he therefore desired to manage it with utmost care.

So it is with money. Your bank account has your name on it,

and perhaps that of your spouse as well. It's yours in every sense of the word. Yet it's when you begin to see yourself as a steward—the manager, not the owner—of your finances that you will start making better decisions with your money.

Servant stewards

The New Webster's Expanded Dictionary defines a steward as "one who manages affairs for another." Think of a steward on a cruise ship or a flight attendant on a plane. Both are there to take care of their passengers, to serve them—and that's how we see our role with our clients. As their stewards, we assume what is called a fiduciary role with those individuals. We are held to a standard of conduct that says we will manage their money in a prudent manner and practice good stewardship of their assets.

We certainly had that responsibility in mind when one of our clients called us with a unique request. He had attended a meeting at an area Christian ministry and decided that he wanted to help raise money for the distribution of the "Jesus" film, a feature movie that depicts the life of Jesus Christ and has been translated into more than 1,600 languages since its original production in 1979. The clients' son was killed in a tragic accident when he was 25, and they wanted to honor his legacy by funding a new language translation of the film. When they shared the amount they wanted to give, it was a significant amount.

"Can we do it?" they asked. Interestingly, they were not only telling us what they were going to do with the money, but they were asking us for permission and an analysis to evaluate if it fit into their overall financial plan.

What a responsibility they were giving us! Yet its one we treasure because of the fact that we see ourselves as trusted servants for our clients. We went right to work, doing the analysis with them right there on the phone. This project was important to them and we wanted to do our best to help them fund their project without impacting their future retirement. As far as they were concerned, their money was God's, not theirs. To put it another way, they were managing God's financial portfolio, not their own.

> As far as they were concerned, their money was God's, not theirs.

It reminds us of the time one of John's friends gave him a Montblanc pen. In case you don't know, these are not your run-of-the-mill writing instruments. A Montblanc pen costs hundreds, sometimes thousands, of dollars. John says that if he holds that pen too tightly in his hand, not wanting to let go, when God wants him to release it into His control, the expensive pen can easily break and hurt his hand in the process. But if he holds the pen with a loose, open hand and turns it over to God, the pen will remain intact, and John will avoid any pain. Being a manager, not an owner, of your finances is sometimes about being willing to let go of your perceived control so that the resources can be used for a greater purpose.

Lessons from history

History tells of an individual who learned he was a manager, not an owner, of the resources he had at his disposal. King David, whose life story is told in several books of the Old Testament of the Bible, conducted a fundraising effort to pay for a massive building program for his son Solomon to fulfill: the construction of a temple to God. The effort ended up being so successful that they reached their goal very early in the campaign.

Can you imagine a pastor getting up in church during the offering and telling the ushers to stop passing the plates because they had already received enough money? We've never seen that happen—but the people of Israel gave so much for the building of the temple that their generosity caused David to break out in praise and gratefulness. His prayer, recorded in 1 Chronicles 29:11-17, recognized that "everything in the heavens and on earth is yours, O Lord." Then, after declaring his belief that wealth and honor come from God alone, who rules over everything, and that God made the people great and gave them strength, he proclaimed, "Everything we have has come from you, and we give you only what you first gave us ... and I have watched your people offer their gifts willingly and joyously."

David's prayer clearly acknowledged his view of God in relation to his resources: "It all belongs to you!" When David spoke this petition of thanksgiving, he was near the end of his life. He understood that nothing he had accumulated was going to go with him when he was gone. It wasn't his to take, and he desired it all to be used for the major objective of building the temple.

Another lesson comes from Hannah, a faith-filled woman who intimately understood what it meant to be a manager, not an owner—of her own son. As told in 1 Samuel 1, she was unable to have a child for years and continuously cried out to God in prayer, promising to dedicate her child to God's service. One day, Eli the priest, seeing her persistence before God, told Hannah, "Go in peace! May the God of Israel grant the request you have asked of him." (1 Samuel 1:17) Not long after, Hannah gave birth to a son, Samuel, and she followed through on her promise to God. She took the child to Eli and left him to be raised in the temple. Samuel went on to become one of the most influential and godly prophets in the Bible, thanks to Hannah's willingness to give God everything, even her own son. In 1 Samuel 2:8 she declared, "For all the earth is the Lord's, and he has set the world in order."

There's a story of a man who was a successful business owner and loved his money so much it was his life's passion. Therefore, before he died, he asked his wife to bury him with his money because it was all that mattered to him. At the funeral, to honor his wishes, she placed a closed shoe box on his chest, visible to all viewing his open casket.

When she sat down, a friend who knew of his wishes questioned, "You didn't really leave his money with him, did you?"

His widow replied, "Yeah. I wrote him a check. If he can cash it, he can take it with him."

Have you ever seen a hearse pulling a U-Haul? Neither have we. The person who dies with the most toys still dies. So, if you can't take it with you, it's wise, as the manager and not the owner, to plan accordingly.

2

- Principle #1 -

Contentment: When Enough Becomes Enough

What amount of money would it take to ensure a life of comfort and fulfillment for the rest of your days? A million? A billion? Pick any number that makes you feel secure.

Now here's the truth: any number you came up with was wrong. Why? The adage, "Money can't buy happiness" is core to the first principle of developing and living a lifestyle of generosity. Money can (and will) only go so far, regardless of how much of it you have. There can never be enough of it. Written by King Solomon, believed to be one of the wisest men who ever lived, Ecclesiastes 5:10 states, "Those who love money will never have enough. How meaningless to think that wealth brings true happiness!"

But there *can* be enough of everything else in your life—and it's when you can start to truly believe that in your heart that you will stop striving for more, begin being grateful for what you already have, and acknowledge that you don't actually need more. Then enough becomes enough. In Philippians 4:11-13, Paul shares a powerful perspective: "Not that I was ever in need, for I have learned how to be content with whatever I have. I know how to live on almost nothing or with everything. I have learned the secret of living in every situation, whether it is with a full stomach or empty, with plenty or little." He then recognized how God is the supernatural force that helped him be content in all of his circumstances.

Yet we see two entirely natural forces competing with the idea of enough being enough. The first is the pervasive advertising industry that screams that having more is the path to happiness. If you have an old Hyundai, you need to buy a new Camry. If you have a new Camry, then you most certainly need a new Audi. And if you own the Audi, well, you can't possibly be content until you have luxury of a Mercedes Benz or the sportiness of a Maserati.

The same is true of smaller, more basic products. A friend recently told us of a commercial he saw for an online service that will allow you to order air filters for your home HVAC units to be delivered to you on a predetermined schedule based on when you needed to change them out. This makes you happier because it saves you the supposedly massive inconvenience of going to the neighborhood store to get your filters when you need them, or of having to actually remember when to switch out the old filters for the new—and it's available, of course, for a nominal monthly fee.

It reminds us of the VeggieTale's episode, *Madame Blueberry: A lesson in…Thankfulness.*[5] If you've never seen it, you should watch it—even if the kids aren't with you. Before the main story begins, the two main characters of the program, Bob the Tomato and Larry the Cucumber, are up on the kitchen counter when Larry interrupts Bob by zooming over to him driving a very pink vehicle.

"Wow! What is this thing?" Bob asked.

"It's my new suzy-action jeep," Larry said with a grin. "I've been wanting it just forever and now it's finally mine."

"Wow! You must be pretty happy to get a cool toy like that," Bob said.

"Oh, yeah. Well, almost," Larry admitted as he got out of the jeep.
"Almost?"

"Well, there's just one more thing I need to be really happy." Larry added, and then went on to tell Bob about the suzy-action camper. "You just hook it up to the trailer hitch on my action jeep and I'll be ready for a weekend of wilderness fun."

That prompted Bob to ask, "So once you get the camper, then you'll be happy?"

"I don't know," Larry said. "There's also the dirt bike."

"The dirt bike?"

"And the jet ski—and the action hang glider."

"Larry," Bob admonished. "How much stuff do you need to be happy?"

"I don't know," Larry said. "How much stuff is there?"

Larry had certainly been influenced by the advertising he saw about suzy-action toys, but he later went on to learn how to be content and grateful for what he already had. Andy Stanley, an author, pastor, and founder of North Point Ministries, said in an October 2018 podcast that he can't imagine how much more he could've saved or given away if someone else hadn't told him about all the stuff he supposedly needed.

The second force after advertising that is even more pervasive for many people is social media. It's taken "keeping up with the Joneses" to a whole new level. The biggest social media platform in the world is Facebook. As reported in Frontline's 2018 documentary *The Facebook Dilemma*, its News Feed uses a secret mathematical formula, an algorithm, to rank content in terms of what is deemed most important to each individual user. It is designed to give you the content you most want to see and keep you scrolling through the feed. Then, the introduction of the Like button allowed the News Feed algorithm to collect vast amounts of users' personal data to further inform the content they receive.

This is how Facebook, and other social media platforms using similar algorithm strategies, know how to send you content that can, if you're not careful, cause you to feel quite a bit of *dis*content—particularly with what you possess. When others post pictures of themselves in their new outfit or wearing those new shoes, or they pass on a link to where they got the new cookware (just in time for the ready-made gourmet meal service they subscribed to), it tempts you to level up. After all, you deserve to get what they have, right? Aren't you worth it?

Roger McNamee, an early Facebook investor who later became a concerned critic of the company, told Frontline regarding Facebook's algorithm, "Polarization was the key to the model—this idea of appealing to people's lower-level emotions; things like fear and anger to create greater engagement and, in the context of Facebook, more time on site, more sharing, and therefore, more advertising value."[6]

> It all starts with determining what *does* fulfill you. What, exactly, is enough?

It's a cautionary tale that encourages you to assess why you use social media, how much you should trust it, and how much weight you should give it in your decision-making. If you allow it to, advertising or any other factor or person may influence how you feel about your stuff (and yourself), causing personal satisfaction to be fleeting. Yet when you come to a realization that you can be happy—or are already happy—with what you have, then the power of those influences is taken away.

It all starts with determining what *does* fulfill you. What, exactly, is enough?

Setting your standard

We know a couple in their late twenties who, even though both were highly-paid professionals, decided that their family of four was going to live at the poverty level. Their income at that time exceeded $100,000 annually, yet they felt God calling them to change their lifestyle to make it on approximately $22,000 each year. (As of 2017, the poverty level for a family of four sits at nearly $34,000; their $100,000 income would now be about $160,000.) Why did they choose to do it? They wanted to give away the balance of their income to support what they believed to be godly causes and ministries. They also desired to teach their children not to be greedy. Sound impossible? They did it—and last we heard, still were.

While we're not suggesting everyone should take such a radical approach to their finances, we are saying that everyone should carefully examine their own lifestyle to be sure that they are living the standard they need or desire for themselves and their families, not the standard dictated by the society around them. Once you set that standard and decide what is enough, you can find contentment in that choice.

The first two expenses to look at as you set your standard are housing and transportation. These are typically the two biggest expenses for most families. If you perceive these two areas are not enough, you will never have enough to become financially secure. Both are extremely expensive transactions. They are also debt-driven transactions. With both, you give yourself permission to live beyond your means—and with both, you're really not buying a home or a car, but a payment: one with interest that most people end up making for years to come.

Certainly, the family who chose to live at the poverty level would've first had to pay off their existing mortgage, downsize to a less expensive home, or rent. With their vehicles, they would've either first paid them off or traded them in for a single used car paid for outright. For you, it could be downsizing from two or more vehicle payments to one, or if your situation allowed it, eliminating your vehicle altogether (along with the insurance payment) and opting for public transportation or a bicycle. With your home, you might refinance your mortgage or sell your home for something different. Finally, you simply might decide that what you already have is enough and forego the planned remodel of the kitchen. Instead you could use that money to create a fund for maintenance and repairs as your home ages. You may also decide the transportation you have is sufficient, meaning that the sedan you have doesn't have to be traded in to get the pricier SUV.

The key is to look at both, set a standard—a lifestyle cap—and agree to it. We recently started working with a couple whose goal was to retire within a few years. In the process of working down their debt, they reduced to one vehicle and made it work, even though both worked in different parts of the city. By doing so, they created the capacity to eliminate their debt faster and be debt-free by the time they quit working.

In Brian's family, he and his wife had the funds to purchase a larger home, but they decided to cap that part of their lifestyle in order to create more travel experiences to enjoy with their children. They discussed it with the kids. "There is a house down the street we could buy right now," they announced, showing them photos of the home. "There's nothing wrong with our current home. It meets our needs, but, if you'd like, we could live in this bigger house, or we could travel more and go with dad on trips when he travels on business." They made their choice—and have since visited places like Miami and Chicago.

This lifestyle cap will vary for different people. It could be two homes and three cars, or six houses and 12 vehicles, or one home and no car. What's important is that you determine it, take the steps to make it a reality, and then be (and remain) content in your decision. Otherwise, you'll have resentment instead of contentment.

We recommend that people begin by taking an inventory of all they are thankful for—family, health, possessions, and personal faith—and rest in that attitude of gratefulness. Then they are positioned to ask themselves some questions to help them set their lifestyle cap:

- What do you value most in your family? Brian's family valued travel experiences over housing. This goes to the core of what you really want. Do you wish to be an average middle class household? Upper middle class? Do you want to keep up with your country club neighbors? As you answer this question, you come to the realization that you can't have it all, which helps you identify what is enough for you.

- How much do you want to allocate toward your priorities? This process allows you to see where you are currently spending too much, or perhaps possess too much, so that you can adjust accordingly. If you want to travel more, for example, will getting rid of one of your cars (and the payment and maintenance that goes with it) allow you to have more funds for trips?

- Are there any changes coming up that could compromise your lifestyle cap? Let's say you have a housing expense cap that works in Albuquerque, New Mexico, but are going to be moving to Los Angeles, California where the cost of housing (and everything else) is much greater. Can you protect your cap? How? Perhaps you are planning to adopt a child. That will increase your overall living expenses. What do you need to adjust?

Your upbringing can also be a factor as you examine these questions. You may have grown up with very little and are therefore comfortable with little. Or, that same background may compel you to want to have a bit more for you and your family. Maybe you want everything for your kids because you had nothing in your childhood. Be aware that your past can positively—or sometimes negatively—impact your lifestyle cap decisions.

Setting your perspective

We prefaced this book with the statement that the United States has never before had more wealth than it does right now. And, to be more precise, most people who live in America have more affluence than they think. Want evidence? Go to www.globalrichlist.com, provided by CARE International. Type in USA in the location selector, then enter your annual net income. If you put in $80,000, for example, you'd discover that someone making that amount in this country is in the top one percent of the richest people in the world. That's top *one* percent. That makes you the 6.2 millionth richest person on earth since it estimates you make over forty dollars an hour.

Compare that to the example it provides of the average laborer in Indonesia who earns just 39 cents per hour.

> Understand that enough is never enough when it comes to money.

That exercise is not intended to make you feel guilty for what you have. Just the opposite, it should give you perspective about the money you earn and the incredible but basic wealth you *do* possess—a roof over your head, a climate-controlled space, transportation, food and supplies—when compared to most other people in the world. It's truly amazing! Hopefully, that perspective will also birth within you a conviction to not only be happier with what you have, but that much more determined to create the lifestyle cap needed to equip you to better manage your finances, your possessions, and become more generous with your giving.

In the end, it's not up to us or anyone else to tell you what you should do. Instead, understand that enough is never enough when it comes to money, take control of the influences that can cause you to feel that you don't have enough, and set the standard for what is enough for you based on having the correct perspective. Then you are able to take ownership of your decisions and find contentment through your choices.

You are also positioned for our next principle: tradeoffs, and developing the financial maturity to give up today's desires for your future benefit.

3

- Principle #2 -

Tradeoffs:
What to Give and Take

I don't know about you, but when it comes to desserts, nothing beats a delicious pie. Whether it's apple (John's favorite) or pumpkin (Brian's preference, complete with candles for his birthday the week of Thanksgiving), a thick slab of pie makes the meal. Just seeing it in the round pan, its sweet scent wafting through the room, makes your mouth water, doesn't it?

Of course, having that tasty slice comes with its tradeoffs. If you're like us, you have to choose to eat less of the entrée that comes before it so that you save room in your tummy for its goodness. Others may have to forego treats all week so that the pie can be eaten and enjoyed.

Tradeoffs are a part of life—and that's never more true than with your finances. But if you look at your life in relation to money as being like a big pie, it can make your management of your finances more understandable and palatable.

Kingdom Advisors (KA) is an organization that trains its members in biblically wise financial advice. It's president, Rob West, hosts the MoneyWise Radio show aired daily nationwide. One of the tools

KA uses is a pie chart that describes five uses of money in four words: Live, Give, Owe, and Grow.

Using this process, we see that everyone's pie is a different size, but there are only five pieces, and knowing how your pie is sliced is the first and most important part of getting control of your finances and heading toward a lifestyle of generosity.

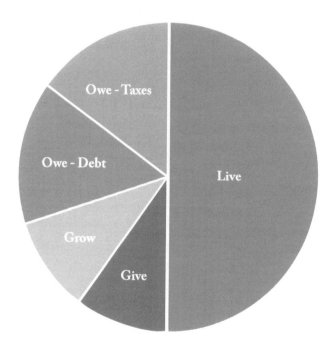

Source: Kingdom Advisors

Live: Typically, this portion takes up half of your pie, and it represents the monthly or annual cost of being you—housing, utilities, clothing, etc.—and it'll vary based on the lifestyle you lead. Believe it or not, using monetary resources for yourself is part of proper biblical financial management. The concept is founded on the surprising scriptural principle of 1 Timothy 6:17, which says our "trust should be in God, who richly gives us all we need for our enjoyment." God actually wants us to be joyful with the resources He provides and to use them for our enjoyment.

Give: Most people assume this slice of the pie only refers to charitable giving, but it represents any money that is going to help other people, including family and friends. When you assume that all of the money you have is for you, that's greed; but when you give, you acknowledge that all of your money is not for you alone. A portion is for others. In general, giving represents 10 percent of your money, but should grow as you better manage the other areas. In the next chapter, we'll talk more about the difference between rules-based giving and true generosity.

God actually wants us to be joyful with the resources He provides.

Owe: This is divided into two slices, taxes and debt. Of course, taxes are mandatory and usually represent no more than 20 percent of your money use, but we like to say that you should pay every dime of tax you owe, but not a penny more. The idea is to take advantage of tax laws and not abuse them through wise tax planning.

When it comes to debt, we've found that most people have never seen all of their debt spelled out at once. If they do, they tend to only see the payments, not the full amounts. You must look at your debt realistically to properly address it. Debt should not represent more than 40 percent of your cash flow, and if you're being squeezed on what you have available in your Live slice, it's usually because of debt.

Grow: This slice of the pie, about 10 percent at the beginning, is money set aside for the future. It could be savings, investments, or a combination of the two. Money that goes into your retirement plan is part of this piece of your pie.

According to financial and investment advisor Ron Blue, two

of the uses (Live and Owe) are consumptive, while Give and Grow will yield a benefit later on. "It is fairly simple," Blue says, "to look at last year's numbers and fill in the blanks for how much owing (both debt and taxes), growing, and giving you did. What remains in your income is what you have left to live on. Knowing this, you are motivated to spend differently so that you have a pie chart that reflects the priorities of your heart."

Blue identifies two things that determine how we allocate our money in the slices of the pie: commitments and priorities. Commitments, he says, come with various family situations and often arise out of past financial decisions. Money put toward debt, for example, has to do with past spending choices. Expenditures on food, clothing, and other daily needs arise from our unique family situations. In both cases, we have differing levels of commitment.

Priorities come into play from our lifestyle decisions. Our choices will leave us with more or less for saving and giving. "Life continually demands that we assess our priorities and make adjustments to our spending decisions accordingly," Blue said. "Having clarity about your priorities and having ongoing reinforcement for the values you hold dear will allow you to make financial decisions that are in line with your priorities."

That's why in the previous chapter we covered the concept of contentment, the first principle, and what is and isn't enough while developing a lifestyle cap. They help you size up your commitments and establish your priorities: the Live piece of the pie. In later chapters, we'll fill out our pie as we look at principles for Give (our four T's of generosity), Owe (featuring our SOAP steps to cleaning up debt), and Grow (where you'll discover how to be a SMILER with your resources, and where we introduce our investment portfolio triangle).

Flipping the script

For many, "budget" is a dirty word, but it shouldn't be. A spending plan equips you with information that then empowers you to manage the contentment-driven lifestyle cap you've chosen. Yet the reality is that some of the couples we've worked with, who are in deep debt and are overspending, are in that situation because they don't want to say "no" to anything. They want their kids to go to private school. They want to travel. They want a nice car and house and clothes. They are checking every box at the top level. They want it easy, they want it now, and they want everything. No limits, and certainly no tradeoffs. That's the culture in which we live.

But we need to be countercultural when it comes to our money. The problem is, we rarely talk about spending plans when we counsel our clients because we've learned that most people are rarely successful in developing a spending plan, much less executing it. That's unfortunate: a spending plan is a great way to understand how to shrink your Live slice when it's too big to allocate funds to the Grow and Give slices.

Therefore, we encourage people to flip the script by focusing on giving and saving first, then learning to live on what's left. Even when someone has a massive debt problem, we still will frequently counsel them to begin giving as an acknowledgement that they are the manager, not the owner, of their money. That's how we position people to establish their lifestyle cap. We believe this is not only the most biblical way to take care of your money, but it's also the most successful.

For example, we might counsel a client by saying, "I see what you earned last year, what you paid in taxes, and what you paid in debt. So, how much more did you save during the year?" For most people, that amounts to very little outside of their retirement plan at work.

Then we can help them "back into" how much they actually spend monthly or annually in the Live slice of their pie. Here's the equation we use:

Income - Owe - Owe - Grow - Give = Live
Annual Income *minus* Owe (taxes from 1040 form)
minus Owe (all annual debt payments)
minus Grow (total savings, usually defined
as the annual contribution to a retirement plan)
minus Give (as taken from the Schedule A itemized deduction)
equals Live

When we pull three numbers from the tax return (income, taxes, giving) and then ask for monthly debt payments and the 401k savings rate, that usually allows us, in just a few minutes, to have all five slices of the pie. In most cases, this is eye-opening, because most people have an inaccurate assumption about what they are spending compared to what they are *really* spending. From there, they can see what their pie looks like and build a plan around that actual Live amount.

One of the families we've been working with for years headed into full retirement knowing they were going to be losing a significant chunk of monthly income. At the same time, they needed to manage the health care costs of their youngest child who was still attending school and needed coverage through them. Because we had been working with the couple to help them develop and understand their pie, they not only had the information they needed to know what slices of the pie were going to have to be adjusted to handle both the income loss and expense increase, they *understood* it—and felt empowered to respond proactively rather than reactively. Caring for their son was their priority, so they looked at their cash flow and determined what slice of the pie had to be used to provide the needed income. They came up with a doable plan to face what otherwise may have been perceived as an overwhelming combination of circumstances.

On the other hand, we've been assisting an affluent couple who wanted to invest $1 million on the remodeling of their house. The obvious quandary was, "Where was the money going to come from?" As we helped them look at their pie, they recognized the modifications they were going to have to make in their Live and Give slices to pay for everything they wanted to do to recreate their home. They also understood that they were going to have to later replenish what they were using for the remodeling project in order to realize their long-term goals.

Therein lies one of the advantages of the Live, Give, Owe, Grow pie. Each person's situation is different. Finding a few hundred dollars a month to cover a child's health care costs versus coming up with $1 million to redesign a home are hardly comparable needs. They're as unalike as apples and oranges, or maybe even apples and walnuts. But the principle employed, and the tool used, is the same—and it works.

The benefits of delayed gratification

Another counterculture move we need to make to live a lifestyle of generosity is to keep our lifestyle in check. This is where tradeoffs, and give and take, matter. We have found that delayed gratification is the tension between Live and Grow, or money used now versus money saved or invested for the future. Many disagreements about money among couples comes when one person thinks the Live portion needs to be bigger while the other feels the Grow or Give slices need to increase. In addition, most people simply don't save enough money. They end

> Tradeoffs, and give and take, matter.

up experiencing "lifestyle creep," the idea that over time our life-style increases until people are in their fifties and they look back and exclaim, "Wow—I haven't saved anything, but remember the house we used to live in? The cars we used to drive?" They almost laugh about how they lived in their twenties, realizing they have increased their lifestyle, but not done anything extra.

We are amazed at how many people we see who have really good incomes but very little savings. There is a hospital CEO we know in her late fifties who has been a medical executive for decades, yet each of us have more savings than her. This blows our mind—but it all comes from the lifestyle choices we make along the way.

It's in the financial planning process where people make tradeoffs, assessing their priorities and figuring out how much is needed to meet those priorities. For example, if someone comes in and tells us they want to retire in twelve years, we will sit down with them and figure out how much they need to Live. Then we can calculate how much they will need to Grow in that time to sustain the lifestyle they want while reaching their goal, and also, decide how to allocate the money and resources they have left.

Just like their situations, the tradeoffs people have to make come in all varieties. We know a couple moving toward retirement who loved their yearly getaways to the red rock cliff vistas of Sedona, Ari-zona. As much as the scenery, they also enjoyed staying at L'Auberge de Sedona, an award-winning resort and nature spa that's anything but light on the pocketbook. They'd been lodging at L'Auberge every time, but a possible tradeoff when using the Live slice to the Grow wedge of the pie example could be to stay at the resort every sec-ond or third year and replace it with a less expensive hotel on the off years. That's an example of delayed gratification that could still allow the couple all the benefits of Sedona itself while putting away a larger sum of money for their retirement.

Another couple we knew who were looking toward retirement was, in many ways, living their retirement lifestyle early, traveling often and regularly buying a new RV for their excursions. However, they wouldn't be able to retire as early as they hoped if they kept up their excursions and RV purchases. They had amazing consensus on their money usage, more than most couples, and in this case, they were in perfect agreement: they wanted to travel as much as they wanted, in the RV they wanted, and still retire when they wanted. They had to choose: did they want to have more money and time to have fun now, or have that time and money later when they retired? They were forced to examine the tradeoffs.

A vital aspect to the Live, Give, Owe, Grow pie is to not only see what it's telling you today, but to discern what it says about one year from now, or three, or five, or 20 years down the road—and then respond to it with delayed gratification today that will harvest full gratification tomorrow. One couple we know built their dream home in Breckenridge, Colorado. They could afford it, but would've had to make a lifestyle change in ten years to continue living there. Discernment was required in order to accomplished what they desired.

Again, everybody's pie is different and must be sliced accordingly based on their goals, priorities, and values. Therefore, if someone values retiring early, their Grow slice will have to get bigger. People involved in the FIRE (Financial Independence, Retire Early) movement are saving up to 70 percent of their income in their thirties so that they can retire by the time they're in their forties.

Yet those who value generosity and want to use their money to care for others will be required to increase their Give slice to match. Only when they do that can they experience the freedom that comes from saving enough—and the joy that comes from giving generously.

4

- Principle #3 -

Giving: Breaking the Power of Money

One of the things Brian has spearheaded to model a lifestyle of generosity to our clients was to create events where they could come together and get to know one another while, at the same time, helping a local organization. Our first such event was for the Roadrunner Food Bank in Albuquerque, New Mexico. It was an opportunity to serve jointly and provide our clients an easy way to give back and have fun at the same time.

Did they ever! We had about 20 clients attend, and together we sorted almost 5,000 pounds of produce to be distributed to needy families. The folks at Roadrunner said it was the most produce ever sorted at one time by a single group. When we were done, all of us ate together from a food truck we hired, thereby blessing a local business, to provide a hot lunch for our clients and all of Roadrunner's employees and volunteers who were present.

What made the event so enjoyable for us is that we gave of our time, used our talents to sort the produce, and gave the treasure of providing lunch for everyone, which made us more thankful for the resources we had.

And there they are—the four "T's" of giving that we are convinced will break the power of money in your life as you learn to give
of it and yourself in the following ways:

- Time
- Talent
- Treasure
- Thanks

Time and Talent

These "T's" are in the same section because the use of talent automatically means the giving of time as well. You can't give one without
the other. Colossians 3:23 encourages us to "work willingly at whatever you do, as though you were working for the Lord rather than for
people." This speaks to the use of both our time and our talents.

Service to your community can give you a great opportunity to
use your skills, and those talents don't have to be what you use in your
vocation. One of John's friends, a pilot with Southwest Airlines, was
also a gifted woodworker. He decided to use that talent to remodel
areas of his church, creating custom cabinets, book racks, and even a
gorgeous pulpit to benefit the church's leaders and the congregation.
He used a talent he wouldn't have otherwise used, and those in his
faith family were blessed by his craftsmanship.

Sometimes the talent you use may simply be to do a needed task.
Years ago, when John was praying about his own personal commitment to service, he noticed how the marquee sign for this church
rarely had clever or encouraging sayings to be read by those passing
by on the heavily traveled road next to the building. It bothered him,
and as he thought about it, he felt God call him to take over the
responsibility of managing the church sign. He volunteered, and care

of the sign and its messaging became an eight-year-long family tradition. He also discovered that if something is really bothering you, that may be the very service God is calling you to do—or the place you are being led to give to—in order to meet that need.

Another aspect about time and talent, in relation to giving, is that it varies depending on your season in life. For example, a golf enthusiast may have a period when he has plenty of time to play, but not enough money to hit the links as often as he'd like. Or he may have enough money to go as much as he'd like, but not enough time to do so. Generosity works that way, too. If you're a college student, you may not have much money, but you may be able to find time on a Saturday afternoon to volunteer. A retired person may not have the physical ability to get their hands dirty at a place like Roadrunner, but they may have more financial resources that they can donate to the organization. There is an ebb and flow that accompanies our different chapters of life.

Assessing your talent also gives you an opportunity to be creative and ask yourself, "What are my God-given gifts or talents?" Most of the time, the things you are good at are also the things that bring you the most joy. It could be your profession, a specific craft, or a passion to care for children. Brian's wife loves to volunteer at their kids' school. It energizes her to be around her children and their classmates. People often think of giving their time or talent as a sacrifice, but it can actually bring much benefit and pleasure to you as the giver.

> Ask yourself, "What are my God-given gifts or talents?"

Finally, when you identify a talent, you should use it. The reason we identify our gifts is to then put them into practice to benefit others. That's why we're given the talent we possess. Therefore, when you feel prompted to give of your time or talent, strive to make sure you've provided enough margin in your life to be able to respond. You want to be able to be impromptu with your generosity.

One young man, Leighton Cusack, applied the "10 second rule" to his giving—meaning that he tried to respond within that quick timeframe to any prompting he received to give. As a high school senior, he acted on one of those urges and decided to give 20-dollar bills to fellow students, with the requirement that they use the money on a random act of generosity. As he began to hear stories from his friends of buying meals for people at restaurants and other kindnesses, Leighton began to understand that no gift was too small or no act of generosity too insignificant. He used the 10 second rule to give himself the room and freedom to be generous, and it changed him and impacted the lives of others.

Treasure

In *Fields of Gold*, Andy Stanley introduced a three-step approach to giving: priority, percentage, and progressive. By this, he encourages people to prioritize their giving by not giving leftovers, to quantify their giving by using a percentage versus an amount, and to give progressively over a long period of time.

It all starts by recognizing that our treasure comes in two general categories: income and assets. You give from a percentage of your income. You can also give from your assets by leveraging advantages in current tax laws and taking a portion of your investments (which, in some cases, can include your retirement savings) to create additional opportunities to be generous. For example, you can give away an asset that has gone up in value and potentially deduct the full value of the asset while not paying the capital gains that you would otherwise pay if you sold the asset yourself. If you have an appreciated stock, you can sell the stock you no longer wish to own and realize the capital gain and the tax that goes with it, or you can give it away and avoid the gain and tax. Yet another option, if you own a piece of property you wish to sell, is to transfer ownership of all or a portion of that property to a charity. Once the property is sold, that cash is freed up to be used by the charity.

Or, if you're a business owner, you could give away a percentage of your company. For example, a potential strategy is for an owner to give 10 percent of his business assets and put it into a donor advised fund at a non-profit, such as the National Christian Foundation. Any time that company paid a dividend, that income was not taxed and was available to give away to ministries. If that company is sold someday, there will be no capital gains tax to that portion of the sale proceeds, and that cash could go to fund ministry work.

The charity gets the donation. The giver avoids tax. The only loser in that strategy is the IRS—and that's okay. We hate sending money on a one-way trip to Washington, D.C.

Here are the four main ways that you can give from your assets:

1. Publicly traded securities
2. Closely held businesses
3. Real estate
4. Retirement accounts or qualified charitable distributions (QCDs)

With QCDs, all charitable distribution after you are 70 years and six months old is allowed to be taken from your IRA and sent directly to a charity. That distribution does not appear as taxable income, but it does satisfy the requirement that you have to distribute a small amount of your IRA every year. Under this strategy, you can give up to $100,000 out of your IRA to charities.

Often, these strategies allow you to reduce the Owe slice of your pie by being wiser with the Give slice. They give you tax benefits and more flexibility with your treasure.

If you are not sure how much to give, "10 plus one" is a great guideline to use. With it, you begin by giving 10 percent of your income and one percent of your assets. Ten percent comes from the biblical principle of the tithe. One percent is a good starting place a family can give from assets, and typically it will not negatively impact their ability to grow their assets and meet other goals. Once you prioritize 10 plus one, you can then apply it to your Live, Give, Owe, Grow pie to determine your regular treasure allocation.

One of the biggest upsides to 10 plus one is that it unlocks the power of giving assets. Over time, most people do not substantially increase on the 10 percent they are giving from their income, but we have seen people move to much higher levels on the asset side very quickly because it is an area they have never considered. Sometimes, it is where the money with the most untapped potential for generosity is located. Donors are urged to consult their attorneys, accountants, or tax advisors with respect to questions relating to the deductibility of various types of contributions to a donor-advised fund for federal and state tax purposes.

Of course, any of these giving strategies in terms of tax savings can be impacted by tax law changes, so consult your tax advisor before making any decisions with your financial advisor.

Starting a habit early of giving of your treasure is important because it is a lot easier to begin giving a generous percentage of your income and assets when the dollar amounts are small, as compared to trying to sacrifice lifestyle choices that you have established later in life. Many folks in their fifties will have an epiphany about giving a higher percentage of their assets, but they find it hard to reverse or unwind a set lifestyle with its monetary demands.

In general, those who are the most successful at being generous have already been giving for a long time. Sometimes they started giving 10 percent of their income by tithing in church when they were children. In fact, it's amazing to us how much generosity was modeled to them by their parents. Many people don't give because they haven't seen, through their childhood experiences, how their families give and still have enough. We've yet to meet anyone who gave so much that they ended up not having enough. In my opinion, it just doesn't happen.

That's why we champion giving and saving first, then learning to live on what's left. That prevents you from giving from your leftover income or assets because you've prioritized generosity to begin with. The Bible calls this "first fruits" giving, a principle that simply says to give *before* you do anything else. When we give to our churches, for example, we make sure it is the first check that we write—and we advocate doing this each time money comes into your bank account. It's a literal demonstration of first fruits giving.

Over the years we've told others, "We've never met a former tither." That's the case because it works. We heard of one woman who threw all the money in her purse into the offering plate, even though she was planning to use the money to go to the grocery store later that day. After she got home, a neighbor asked if she could babysit and paid her the exact amount that she gave that morning, allowing her to go to the store as planned.

First fruits giving is one of the few places in Scripture where God actually throws out a challenge. In Malachi 3:10, God says, "I will open the windows of heaven for you. I will pour out a blessing so great you won't have enough room to take it in! Try it! Put me to the test!" We even heard of one church that gave its members a money back guarantee. If they tried tithing for 90 days and didn't feel like they had been blessed, the church returned the donations to the giver.

Families don't always see eye to eye on giving. There are times a spouse may be hesitant, for example, to take the leap of faith tithing requires, or perhaps one member of the couple is just naturally more generous than the other. There are many instances where we have seen others give back, such as one person who gave their newlywed daughter and son-in-law a monetary wedding gift to help them start their new life together. The daughter then gave a portion of that gift to her church. We don't want people to give just because they will receive or because there is a guarantee they will get their money back, but we've seen things like this happen time and again for those who have committed themselves to first fruits giving.

Another saying we have in terms of first fruits generosity is "do your givin' while you're livin' so you're knowin' where it's goin'." Sometimes people choose to give from their estates after they are deceased because they are concerned that if they give while they are alive, they won't have enough to live on. But we think that robs them of the joy of giving. Obviously, we don't discourage estate plan gifts because they are a wonderful opportunity to be generous—but we simply believe it is better to give while you are alive so that you can see it at work, enjoy the tax benefits, see the impact on the community, and be able to monitor the recipient, whether it is a family member or a charity.

Rather than give a charity a million dollars when you are dead, for example, why not give them several thousand dollars a year now and see how they use it to change people's lives? Instead of leaving your children a trust, why not give them money and teach them what to do with it? Some of our clients do that by setting up a charitable fund, encouraging their kids to give into it, and then sharing with the family the amount they chose and why. Ron Blue says money can be used as a tool (for yourself, say, to finance a vacation, or for others by giving to a charity), a test (such as with children to see how they use it, or with a not-for-profit organization to see how it invests it), or a testimony (giving as a profession of your faith or to help your children achieve their goals). In the end, there are a lot of great ways to use your money while you are alive.

All of this can be a little fearful at first. But once you start, you experience the joy of sharing your treasure—and that joy can become almost addictive. Once people start being generous, they typically don't go back. Pastor and author Rick Warren (most famous for *The Purpose-Driven Life*) recently shared with his church that his generosity has progressed to where he is now giving 90 percent of his income and assets and living on the remaining 10 percent. A similar extravagant example comes from R.G. LeTourneau, the inventor of earthmoving machinery whose story was captured in *Mover of Men and Mountains*. He, too, set aside 90 percent of his salary and company profits and gave it to Christian charities, and then lived on the other 10 percent. Both show the potential of how far you can go with your giving and still have more than enough to live on.

> Once people start being generous, they typically don't go back.

Finally, we've heard it said that any gift can make you a giver, but to be generous the gift needs to be sacrificial. In other words, it is charitable to give the worst suit in your closet to a clothing drive, but it is generous to give your best suit. Rather than giving the leftovers, we encourage clients to give something that is actually of value. Ron Blue tells of the time he and his family decided to forego the cost of their next vacation in order to fulfill a giving obligation they had already made to a charity. Guess what happened? Not long after they cancelled their getaway, a representative from a different not-for-profit organization called and asked if he could travel to speak at one of their events—and bring the family along with him. Through that trip, they ended up getting a vacation after all. They made the initial sacrifice and received an unexpected blessing in return.

Whatever you end up doing, start giving of your treasure. You'll never be the same once you do.

Thanks

So much of our joy or despair about money comes from our perspective. Coming at things from a thankful mindset helps us see an opportunity in places that we might otherwise see something detrimental. For example, many people dread Tax Day. That mid-April due date is almost always viewed with disdain—or worse.

But we believe you should write your annual or quarterly owed tax checks with a grateful heart. Why? Because the fact that you are paying tax means that your execution of Live, Give, Owe, Grow has created enough provision to warrant the payments from your prosperity, as fueled by your generosity and your specific investment opportunities. When Brian paid more in annual taxes than he made in income his first year in the finance industry, he considered it a milestone. He was grateful because he knew the payment was proof that his business had grown and was continuing to expand. We'll revisit this concept regarding taxes in the next chapter.

We also encourage clients to be thankful for volatility in the financial markets. Again, that may sound crazy, especially to those who have conservative or moderate investment portfolios, but down markets can often present buying opportunities that can result in higher returns later. For example, the return on stocks have been greater historically than that from less volatile assets. John's wife, Connie, likes to say that stocks are the only thing people don't want to buy when they are on sale in a down market, yet she began buying stocks through her parents with her babysitting money when she was growing up. As we learn to look at market uncertainty for the opportunities it represents, then negative news becomes positive—and that attitude shift reduces your stress about national or international financial turbulence you feel powerless to control.

It's an entire change of your mindset to think that volatile markets represent opportunity and paying taxes represents provision. Then again, that's exactly what thanks does. It creates a whole new attitude about how you view life that echoes the words of 1 Thessalonians 5:16-18: "Always be joyful. Never stop praying. Be thankful in all circumstances, for this is God's will for you."

As we mentioned earlier in "Introducing the Lifestyle," generosity is born out of contentment and gratitude. One of our favorite biblical principles says to give thanks in all circumstances. We truly believe that. Every Thanksgiving when his kids were younger, John and his family went around the dinner table and had each person, starting with the letter A, declare something that they were thankful for. While the letter X proved problematic, everyone came up with something—and it taught everyone in his family to be grateful. By the time they were having dessert, the entire family was joyful and laughing. John's wife, Connie, routinely sends "thank you" notes to anyone who gives them a gift. Brian says "thank you" to security agents at the airport.

As we declare and practice thankfulness, it will automatically and positively affect your outlook on money. That's a good thing—since our next topic, debt, requires all the grateful thinking we can muster.

5

- Principle #4 -

Debt: Using SOAP to Clean Up What You Owe

Debt is a matter of the heart, not of the wallet. All too often, we see people fall into debt because of things that have nothing to do with money. They may want an expensive sports car because it makes them feel cool, or, as we mentioned earlier, they may want to keep up with the Joneses by constantly remodeling their home or accessorizing their wardrobe. These feelings and attitudes are what put them into debt, not solely the lack of available funds to get what they wanted.

Of course, there are more valid heart reasons that cause debt. One family we work with had one daughter who needed financial help to deal with an unexpected pregnancy, then later aided another child in launching her college education. In both cases, they felt they had no choice but to use debt to meet those needs, and they are still paying off those expenditures (with interest) today.

Whatever the case, we usually don't think of the consequences of how long it will take to pay off the debt, or of what it will do to us. In trying to meet needs or fix problems, the debt ends up causing more problems that take a toll on our well-being. We had one prospective client whose wife incurred significant credit card debt on cosmetic surgery because they had recently lost a child. She spent money she didn't have as a form of dealing with grief, which is extremely common. Many dealing with loss simply stop paying attention to their money for a while and unwittingly accumulate debt.

Debt can certainly be detrimental—but it is a reality for everyone. When we look at debt from a biblical standpoint, Romans 13:8 states, "Owe nothing to anyone—except for your obligation to love one another." The first portion of that verse, however, has often been misappropriated to communicate that debt is wrong when its actual context is to not let any debt remain outstanding. The real problem isn't borrowing, but not paying off the debt. We want to make sure our debts are eliminated so that they're not encroaching on our ability to be generous and content with our finances. Some people come to us carrying a huge weight of guilt because they've been told debt is evil or that its even a sin to have debt. That's unfortunate because Scripture also declares that "there is no condemnation for those who belong to Christ Jesus." (Romans 8:1)

Debt, therefore, is not prohibited in the Bible, but it is viewed as problematic, and there are cautions about it and principles for dealing with it. Once debt is taken on, it is to be paid off. A couple of friends of ours chose to go into bankruptcy to relieve their debt pressure, but they still paid off their creditors, to the tune of several hundred thousand dollars, even though they were no longer under obligation to do so. The bankruptcy declaration gave them time to reorganize things and work with those they owed.

That's a genuine commitment to take care of debt that fed their desire not to get into that dire situation again.

Don't presume

The perfect biblical passage about presumption is James 4:13-15. "Look here, you who say, 'Today or tomorrow we are going to a certain town and will stay there a year. We will do business there and make a profit.' How do you know what your life will be like tomorrow? Your life is like the morning fog—it's here a little while, then it's gone. What you ought to say is, 'If the Lord wants us to, we will live and do this or that.'"

It's a poignant principle, because every time you borrow money, you are making a presumption on the future, assuming you will have the money needed to pay it off. Put another way, you are committing your future self to pay for today's expenses. That may not be the easiest thing to imagine, since there's no way you can know exactly what your circumstances and challenges are going to be 10 years from now, much less two or three. But that is exactly what you are doing. The lender, of course, makes the same presumption. Problem is, your earning power is not guaranteed. All manner of circumstances can—and usually do—happen that either decrease the amount of money you have on hand or increase the amount of funds necessary to meet your wants or needs. Unexpected expenses abound. Plus, you may have prioritized funds for a future goal, but find that goal is now undermined because you used that money today for something else. Presuming on the future is always risky.

> Every time you borrow money, you are making a presumption on the future.

It can catch up with you, too. A new study by Global Atlantic Financial Group,[7] a financial services firm, indicated that 39 percent of Americans are spending more than they budgeted for and 49 percent of pre-retired consumers aged 40 and up believe planning for retirement is more difficult for them than it was for their parents. Even more, Global Atlantic reported, "the fact that retirees spend less than non-retirees may not be by choice, as more than half of retirees have retirement planning regrets of not saving enough, relying too much on Social Security, and not paying down debt before retiring."

The study added that women (62 percent) are more likely than men (42 percent) to have regrets connected to not saving enough, in part because of having to pay off too much debt.

Does that mean we are to never borrow money? In today's society, that's next to impossible. Few families have cash available, for example, to fully pay for the purchase of a house. But we like to say that the American Dream is to own a home, not buy one. That requires you to decide and diligently plan to get rid of the obligation. Likewise, we discourage using debt or a credit card to pay for depreciating assets. When we pay for a meal on a card, for example, that depreciates very quickly. The same is true of a vehicle. A good question to ask yourself is, "What passions or opportunities am I not pursuing today because of my current debt?" Few people look at the debt they are now paying and consider if there are better places to use that money. Yet there are many things we buy with debt that really have no lasting value at all but that we will end up paying for in the future.

Think about this: in order for you to pay off $1.00 in debt, you probably have to earn between $1.20 and $2.00 in income to pay it off. When you have to make a $500 payment every month, you are presuming that you will be able to earn somewhere around $750-$1,000 dollars a month to make that payment. Yet we rarely think of debt with that perspective. In fact, we have become so numb to paying debt we usually have no idea how much it is hurting or restricting us. We simply assume we will always make debt payments because our culture has made consumer debt the norm.

Credit card companies are as diligent as ever in trying to get you to use debt. Many of our clients have told us of receiving credit card offers in the mail that include a check. Depending on which check you write in response, you can get an interest-free or very low interest loan—both of which essentially go on your card balance. However, if you don't pay off that loan within the timeframe you agreed to, you'll pay interest in arrears. You may not know that, though, because that provision is tucked away in the fine print no one reads—and don't expect to receive any wiggle room if you're late. Years ago, John purchased a $900 bicycle from a dealer, and accepted their offer to pay for it deferred within 90 days without paying any interest. The deadline fell on a Saturday, but John paid on Monday, just two days later. The finance company still charged him a hefty retroactive interest of 21 percent for paying late.

"Even the IRS gives you the weekend," John frustratedly told the finance company's representative on the phone, referring to the annual Tax Day deadline. "Well," the person responded matter-of-factly, "we're not the IRS." He then referred John to the back page of the contract, paragraph 17, where it stated that if the deadline fell on a weekend, the payment was due on Friday.

Remember, even the most honest bank or lender has a built-in conflict of interest because they profit from your debt. The more you're in debt and the more interest you pay, in arrears or otherwise, the more money they make.

Relationship realities

Another caution regarding debt is that it can come between you and your most treasured relationships. This is especially true in marriages. Sadly, we've seen divorces happen because couples couldn't resolve their differences or deal with the stress caused by borrowing and debt. We've also seen husbands and wives who are very much in sync in every area of their life, but during our financial planning conversations we discovered that one spouse has been hiding a debt from the other. That is an area of intense shame where lies, dishonesty, and deceit are inserted into an otherwise stable relationship.

We often teach married couples to adopt a simple guideline: if they believe it is going to take credit to buy something they want, wait one day before they actually purchase it. We were teaching a class with other financial advisors, and a person told the story of a time he needed to buy an upgraded printer for a big proposal he needed to produce. The next day, he received an outstanding payment from a client for a fee that he had already written off because he never expected to get paid. The check was for the exact amount of the cost of the printer. The wait-a-day principle allows you the opportunity to see if another solution presents itself. Often, one will—and you won't need to use debt to get something that could place added strain in your home.

As they do with many other aspects of life, we've found that men and women think differently about finances. Men tend to see money like a river, seeing the cash flow of the present and how it runs into the future. Women, on the other hand, usually view money like a lake, a limited reservoir where they can see everything available in one, sweeping glance. Both viewpoints are valid and vital, and when a couple works together to see how the river runs into the lake, they are able to understand each other's perspectives better and improve their debt management.

In general, debt includes mortgage and car payments, consumer debt, and other loans such as student financial aid. Here are three good rules of thumb when it comes to considering your debt. By staying in these parameters, you'll free up enough in your Live, Give, Owe, Grow pie to pay your taxes, give, and save:

1. When purchasing a car, shoot to purchase it for no more than three times your monthly income. So, if you're monthly income is $5,000, spend no higher than $15,000 for a vehicle. Obviously, that means you'll either be buying a used car versus a new one, or you'll be financing a new car with a higher

monthly payment that might compromise other Live, Give, Owe, Grow priorities. Remember that a car, no matter how nice it is, is an immediately depreciating asset, so buying a less expensive vehicle allows you to either pay cash or walk away with a small payment that won't negatively impact your ability to save. If you do finance, do your best to keep it at a reasonable monthly amount.

2. When buying a home, aim to purchase it for no more than two to three times your annual income. A $100,000 a year household income, then, means you could buy a home valued up to $300,000—but be sure to assess taxes or interest rates that might decrease the total cost you can afford. We've seen that most people overextend themselves on mortgage payments and don't have enough money set aside for maintenance of the house, so they end up using consumer debt to pay for those costs.

3. Your overall debt owed should total no more than 40 percent of your monthly take home pay. Most couples who are in trouble with debt are paying out more than that. For example, the earlier couple with the $80,000 credit card debt were paying over $4,000 per month on those cards—fully half of their monthly income. We often see other families paying more each month on consumer debt than they do on their mortgage.

As we've said before, these directives are countercultural. We know that—but they have to be in order to overcome the crisis we're experiencing in our nation today where people simply can't afford what they have. It's not because they don't have income. It's simply that they've overextended themselves. The average person doesn't have enough retirement savings, has too much debt, isn't giving, and is under extreme financial stress. But we don't want you to be average when it comes to your money and your future.

> We don't want you to be average when it comes to your money and your future.

Openly and determinedly addressing your debt can make a positive, joyful difference in your relationships. Of all the wonderful things we get to do with our clients, one of the best is when we celebrate paying off debt. It's amazing the joy a couple feels after paying off their mortgage or when we help them develop a plan designed to help eliminate their accumulated credit card debt, and they begin to implement it. This may sound crazy, but it's often greater than the joy felt when giving large charitable gifts, starting retirement, or even the birth of a grandchild. Why? These large debts weigh on a couple, especially women who are generally more bothered by the debt than their husbands. Yet the feeling of relief knowing it has been paid off or is going to be eradicated is visible. You can see it in their body language and on their faces.

This is an intuitive, natural reaction that is universal and significant when we relieve ourselves from debt. We believe there is something in all of us that tells us we should not be beholden to anybody else. There is also a freedom that comes from it as we are finally released from a spending decision that we made a long time ago. Debt is often associated with regret. When we can get ourselves away from it, there is joy! We don't understand how wonderful it is until we experience it.

Cleaning up your debt with SOAP

As with anything you want to get done, addressing your debt requires intentionality and action—and we believe you can clean it up and keep your finances nice and tidy if you use a little SOAP.

The "S" in SOAP stands for **spending audit**, which allows you to come to grips with exactly how much money you spend and where you spend it. The Bible speaks about this in a common-sense way, telling of a man who wanted to build a tower, then saying, "But don't begin until you count the cost. For who would begin construction of a building without first calculating the cost to see if there is enough money to finish it?"[8] The principle is clear. You should look carefully at the financial aspects of any project before you get too far along in the planning.

The spending audit does this, and despite the connotations of its name, it is relatively easy to accomplish. Using a small, spiral-bound notebook that fits in your pocket or purse, write down every dime you spend—cash, check, or charge. Doing this will give you data on exactly where and how you are spending your money. If you are married, both you and your spouse should do this at the same time. If you're single, find a trusted friend with whom you can share your expenses and be held accountable.

There are apps you can use to automate this process, but we see three downsides to an electronic tool versus old-fashioned paper and pen. One, the app may not catch all of your cash expenditures using money you get from the ATM or cash back at the store. Second, there's just something about writing things down that helps you acknowledge the expense and better retain the information. Third, many apps gather and sell your personal information to third parties, some of which will then offer additional products to you associated with creating more debt. Whatever methodology you choose, though, the point is to do some sort of thorough itemizing.

Then, once a week, sit down and summarize where your money is going. You're looking for leakage: the surprise, automatic, or sometimes even embarrassing spending decisions that are busting your spending plan. One of our clients found he was spending $20.00

a day—a *day*—on Starbucks drinks before, during, and after work. That's $100 a week, at least $400 a month, on an extremely depreciating asset.

This information, vital as you design a spending plan via your Live, Give, Owe, Grow pie, also creates a level of transparency, particularly for couples who don't keep the same bank account. It causes them to acknowledge that their financial destiny is tied together, even if their accounts are not. Whether or not it's "his" money or "her" money, the outcome of their spending decisions are shared. It fosters honest conversation and a willingness to change through healthy conflict and resolution. That's good for every relationship, and it helps make sure your spending choices reflect the values of your family.

Finally, this exercise is not about being perfect. It's about understanding how you are spending your money. One couple we work with keeps separate accounts because he likes to fly airplanes while she loves yoga. So, he spends more than she might think is reasonable on renting aircraft, while she pays more for yoga pants than he ever would on similar clothing. But they are aware of each other's spending, don't judge, and their finances are in good order. Then, when extra expenses came into play because they decided to have children and she became pregnant, they were able to cut back on those non-necessities to prioritize getting ready for the birth of the baby.

The "O" in SOAP instructs you to **organize** your debts by getting them all down in one place. List the lender, the amount you owe, the current interest rate, and the monthly payment. This small, yet key, step will help you put things in proper perspective. Again, an app can certainly aid you with this process, as will a simple spreadsheet. Your debts and other expenditures can be kept in the same file, but you want to have a separate line item for the debts. Most people we've worked with have never seen their debts expressed all in one place at one time, and it can be a jaw-dropper. Again, laying everything out on the table like this can cause honest and potential difficult conversations about your debt and expenditures, especially for couples. But we believe it's better to confront these issues now when you can do something about it rather than later in divorce court when it's too late to make a difference.

Next, you'll take that and carefully design your spending plan for the dollars you have available to you. Look at it as a set of pre-made spending decisions. All you are trying to do is anticipate expenditures before they happen and minimize impulse spending. Basically, the idea is if you haven't made a decision to spend money before you start shopping, don't spend it.

> If you haven't made a decision to spend money before you start shopping, don't spend it.

The "A" in SOAP is for **attack!** You must accept the fact that getting out of debt may require drastic action. It all goes back to tradeoffs and being willing to engage in give and take. Some people want to pay off their debt but not give anything up—but attacking debt will require sacrifices in other areas. Think of this process as warfare: a battle for your financial freedom. Stop thinking of your debts as separate payments and treat all of your debts as *one amount* that is owed. Then, when one debt is paid off, take the payment from that debt and apply it to the next debt on the list. Many people think that when one debt is paid off, they can then buy something else with the money freed up from the debt. But treating all your debts as one payment and one total debt changes that, and greatly accelerates the repayment of the next debts.

The order of repayment is also important. You might think the logical approach is to pay off the highest interest rate debt first. For many people, though, the highest interest rate debt may also be one of the larger debts. The secret is cash flow. You must free up cash flow from one payment so it can be used on the next debt. To do this, you pay off the *smallest* debt first regardless of the interest rate. That frees up the payment from the smallest debt to be unleashed on the next smallest debt. Once both are paid off, you now have the cash flow from the two debts to attack the third debt.

Financial expert and radio show host Dave Ramsey refers to this as the debt snowball method. Some also recommend giving yourself a carrot stick, a small, one-time reward, with each debt that gets eliminated from the snowball. If you were paying $100 a month on something you just paid off, for example, use that amount for a celebration, then add the $100 to the next debt in the snowball. Maybe it's a special dinner out or a weekend getaway. Whatever it is, you'll be using money already in your spending plan so that you don't use money committed toward paying off debt.

It's good to celebrate financial victories along the way. It encourages you and helps you to remain diligent. There is also a sense of freedom that comes with each debt that is paid off that will motivate you to continue versus becoming discouraged by attacking a big mountain of debt and never feeling like you're getting anywhere. You'll become more convinced about paying off debt as you clear each balance and never have to deal with that account again.

Lastly, the "P" in SOAP is to **pay cash** for everything. This automatically implies that you will break the habit of using borrowed money for daily spending. An additional side benefit is that paying cash is an effective way to reduce your overall expenditures.

An example of how this strategy could work would be a couple who committed to paying cash for everything for one full year. They bought gas, groceries, lunches, and any other routine purchase only with money on hand. Credit cards and checks were not allowed.

Interestingly, they found that spending two $20.00 bills was more difficult than writing a $40.00 check, and certainly harder than putting $40.00 on a credit card. The psychological impact of spending cash was significant. It made them carefully think through each purchase. If they didn't have sufficient money in their wallet or pocketbook for the purchase, it had to be postponed until they could go to the ATM. Frequently, purchases that were postponed just never ended up happening. Somehow, those expenditures lost their importance if they had to go back a second time.

Today, of course, few people even use cash, and some places won't even take paper currency or coin any longer. Still, we believe a shorter-term exercise of using cash is a great way to change how you use your money, then determine how you can translate those disciplines to the way you use your debit card that draws money solely from your checking account.

In the end, the goal of SOAP is to change how you make spending decisions by changing behaviors and breaking habits that placed you into debt. It's a matter of the heart. Once you understand why you are making your financial decisions and the motivation behind them, be it spiritual or any other factor, you can then accept that, take ownership to change your behavior—and start living a lifestyle of generosity and true prosperity.

6

- Principle #5 -

Growing:
Having a "Why" Mindset

So far, we've talked about principles to help you manage your expenses today to Live and Give, and we've provided direction on how to address your past spending decisions to take care of the taxes and debt you Owe.

But taking care of the Grow portion of your pie is all about the future: how you use and invest your money in ways that'll impact what you can do for yourself and for others through your generosity.

We could write several books on investing and still not capture all of the concepts we could share on the subjects, be it stocks, bonds, mutual funds, certificates of deposit, or any other number of securities. Yet *The Almighty & the Dollar: A Lifestyle of Generosity* was never intended to be a book about investing. Rather, we are going to focus on the "why" of growing your money rather than the "how." After all, the Grow slice is not just about making more money. If you don't have a reason to grow your money, then what you're doing is nothing more than greed—and despite what you might remember from fictional character Gordon Gekko in the movie *Wall Street*, greed is not good.

Successful investors don't grow their money for the excitement of it. They are not there to raise their blood pressure or to give them something to talk about at the next cocktail party. Truly successful investors grow their money for a specific purpose they can see in the future. For them, it's all about steady wealth accumulation, not the next big millionaire stock.

We believe in helping people set specific goals for their money and then allowing those goals to drive the saving or investment process. We want you to be prepared for milestones in life that may require more flexibility and resources to achieve and, therefore, more assets to accumulate. Those phases might include purchasing a home, funding your children's education, or making a large purchase such as a special trip or a recreational vehicle. It could also include the more common goal of financial independence, having enough money to decide how you want to retire and spend your time later in life. As we noted in Chapter 3, those in the Financial Independence, Retire Early movement are saving large amounts of money each month so that they can retire by the time they're in their forties. It's never too early (or too late) to set saving or investing goals and start pursuing them.

We'll cover some keys to great goal setting later in this chapter—but first we want to align how you perceive your savings and investments, so you can reach those goals. Let's say you need to set aside $50,000 to support your kid's college expenses in the next 10 years. Your "why" is obvious and solid: you desire to help your children, so they won't have to carry student loan debt into their careers and family life. But what about your overall mindset toward growing your money?

We've found that, generally speaking, men are more focused on the process of wealth accumulation while women are more concerned about whether there is plenty available for growth rather than in the process or the specific details of the investments themselves. During our initial meetings with couples, it's not uncommon for the wife to focus on the bigger picture while the husband asks more questions about the portfolio itself, and once both are comfortable one spouse may become less engaged. That's okay, but it's important for both to remain involved, even if it's nothing more than knowing how their money is being handled in case something happens to one of them. After all, both of their viewpoints are vital to facilitate ongoing interaction and dialogue about their finances, and to maintain a good process for their investing while keeping an eye on whether or not they are on track. We've found that couples who save and invest with a *purpose* tend to be more involved and have complimentary mindsets as opposed to a husband and wife who are neither goal nor process oriented.

> We've found that couples who save and invest with a *purpose* tend to be more involved and have complimentary mindsets.

With their perception of savings and investments established, there are some universal directives we give people when it comes to potentially growing their money.

1. **If you have a retirement plan at work that offers a match, put in at least enough to receive it.** Many employers offer a matching contribution for workers who placed part of their salary into a retirement plan. Don't miss this opportunity. This is essentially "free" money from your employer. For many people, this is the sole way they fill their grow bucket early in their lives—and that's vital, because you generally need to plan to have as much as 30 more years of money available to you after you retire, regardless of your age when you start saving or investing.

2. **Diversify your investments because the future is uncertain.**
Generally, the only way to achieve long term returns on your
portfolio is to take some level of risk. Christ's parable about
the three servants in Matthew 25:14-30 provides a great
story about risk. In the end, the servants who were rewarded
by their master were the ones who invested the money they
were given and saw a return on their investment. Still, many
people think of risk as being similar to going to a casino to
double your money or lose it all, but that's not what we are
talking about when it comes to investment risk. The only way
to grow money beyond a minimal risk-free return is to take
risk. Diversification, a strategy that mixes a wide variety of
investments within a particular financial portfolio, helps you
manage that risk so you don't have total loss and experience
the full brunt of typical market volatility. We believe diversification aligns with the biblical principle found in Ecclesiastes
11:1-2. "Send your grain across the seas, and in time, profits will flow back to you. But divide your investments among
many places, for you do not know what risks might lie ahead."
　　We liken it to driving on a washboard gravel road. The ride
is going to be bumpy, but it's a lot more comfortable with shock
absorbers than no shocks at all—and diversification is what
makes the journey through volatility more tolerable. There will
always be a part of your portfolio that you won't like because it
is not doing as well as another part of the investment mix. But
that's actually an accurate measure of proper diversification. If
you are *not* unhappy with something, you're not doing it right.

3. **Stick to your plan in spite of volatility.** The key to doing this
is having a long-term time horizon. Imagine being on a sail-
boat heading out into the open ocean. As the boat rocks over

the waves, it's easy to feel nauseous. But if you look toward a fixed point on the horizon instead of the boat itself, it'll help to provide a less queasy ride. The same is true with market and investment volatility. You have to focus on the time horizon in the future and remember that's where you are going. Matching contributions from your employer may be subject to a vesting schedule. Please consult with your financial advisor for more information.

Often, the best way to think about something long-term is to not think about it right now. When the markets were down and financial statements arrived in the mail, John's wife, Connie, often advised John, "Don't open them. You know it's going to be bad, so just don't open them." It's not that you're ignoring the situation; rather, you are acknowledging that the statement reflects the situation right *then*, but you continue to focus on the long term. During the economic crisis of 2007-2008, we actually witnessed people become physically ill when the bottom fell out of their savings and investments. Some bailed out of the market and never returned—but those who stayed focused on the long term, even during that trying time in our nation's financial history, likely recovered and saw their money grow.

We recall one woman who called us, saying she was scared from watching the financial news on CNBC.

"Why don't you watch the Food Network instead," we advised.

"I like the Food Network," she replied, her voice more upbeat.

"That's the point," we said. "Change the channel."

It seems an easy solution, but it is often hard to do. Yet simply focusing on something else is the best choice.

4. **Automation and rebalancing.** Again, sometimes the best
   thing to do with your money during volatility is nothing at
   all. Stay with your plan—and a great way to ensure you do
   just that is to *automate* as much as possible. Every time you
   make a decision, there is a chance to make a mistake. Save
   an automatic amount every month, either through your
   employer's plan or through an automatic deduction from your
   checking account. You should either have the management
   of your investment process delegated to a professional that
   uses a process, or you should have it automated so you are not
   making decisions that will automatically bring your emotions
   into it. There is always a tendency to chase what is doing well
   and abandon what is doing poorly, and your odds for success
   greatly increase when you use a predetermined process.

   Automation should include the process of putting a predetermined amount of money in savings (per pay period,
   monthly, or every three months), and not just saving when
   you think the market is a good value. Some refer to this as
   paying your investing "bill," treating it like a payment to the
   local electric company. It's not optional. We also look at it
   as paying your future-self first by using the predetermined
   process you have established. In addition, you should *rebal-
   ance* your portfolio regularly. We have found that once a year
   works well. This means you are regularly taking money from
   the winning investments and giving it to the losers, forcing
   you to sell high and buy low. Please note that rebalancing a
   non-retirement account could be a taxable event that may
   increase your tax liability. Most retirement plans now have
   investment alternatives that do the rebalancing for you. It's
   all on autopilot. This prevents you from being influenced by
   financial media and then changing specific stocks, bonds, or

other assets on the fly in a way that could negatively impact your long-term strategy.

If you think this sounds like it'll require you to give up some control of your money, you're right—and that's another mindset adjustment that forces you to focus on the "why" rather than the "how" of growing your money. As people, we are not wired to be good savers or investors. While we automatically flee from most hurtful things such as a needle or a hot oven, many of us are drawn into the fear created by market volatility because we don't know what's going to happen next if we don't respond right away. When things are going well with our money, our brain releases chemicals that send us on a euphoric high, but when we lose money, it's as though we are being held over a cliff and are about to fall. Fear dictates us and we're compelled to do something to fix the problem quickly. Yet that reflex response is counterproductive when it comes to dealing with money, especially in the markets.

The key isn't in avoiding such emotions, but in understanding that they exist and not being dependent on those emotions which lead us astray when it comes to investment decision making. Emotions will come. Having a process allows us to react prudently and increases the chances of being correct. Investor, economist, and professor Benjamin Graham was right when he said, "The investor's chief problem—and even his worst enemy—is likely to be himself."

Goals: Bringing direction to your mindset

Without goals, decisions are made on emotion and short-term thinking. Whether it's about health, relationship issues, or finances, short-term, emotional decisions tend to get us into trouble. Some people think of goal setting as an exercise in inspiration, something that's fancy or froufrou and nothing more. Yet goals are vital, and when it comes to finances, we need to have the long-term in mind.

One of the benefits of a long-term plan is that it helps to prevent a FOMO mentality (fear of missing out) that compels you to pursue something that may have nothing to do with what you are trying to accomplish. So many people, for example, will tell us they want to prepare for retirement but don't because they are using their money to keep up with the Joneses out of fear of missing out on something they have or get to do. The problem is that our perception of what they have or do overrides what's really important. Your friend has a new car, so you go ahead and get one, too, but that's not your goal. Getting about of debt is. FOMO overrules the values that should be driving your goals.

So, how do you start setting long-term goals? Begin by taking a *look at your priorities through the grid of your values.* If you're a couple, ask each other:

- "What are our values?"
- "What are our priorities from those values?"
- "What do we know to be true?"
- "What influences how we make decisions?"

Ron Blue likes to say the only certainty is uncertainty, but don't allow uncertainty to keep you from acting. If you make your decisions about your future based on what you know to be true and you have consensus, you won't require certainty anyway because you'll feel confident that you are on the right track and won't have regrets later.

Your goals should reflect your values, but if you're not careful, your goals can be driven instead by the values and priorities of others. People have come to us who were saving for retirement when they clearly didn't want to retire. Others said how much they loved their church or a charity, but they weren't giving anything. They were repeating what they saw others doing, and their values and actions weren't in agreement.

Therefore, if family is important to you, then education funding for your kids, money to care for an aging parent, or saving for travel experiences could be among your financial goals. They are priorities in alignment with what you value the most. Any spending decisions that are not in alignment with your shared family values will bring confusion, frustration, or resentment.

Money is a tool to help you achieve your goals.

Remember, making money is not a goal. Earning a high rate of interest is not a goal. Those are both ways to achieve a goal, but the goals themselves are things you want to accomplish that originate from your values. Money is a tool to help you achieve your goals. It doesn't give you happiness, but it can help you have or do things that can make you joyful.

Once you have those values-driven priorities in mind, you want to then come together to brainstorm ways to make those priorities into *specific, measurable goals*. Perhaps you've heard of the SMART acronym: specific, measurable, achievable, relevant, and time-based. It's a simple tool used by businesses to go beyond the realm of fuzzy goal-setting into an actionable plan for results—and you can also use it to execute your Live, Give, Owe, Grow pie.

Using a broad goal of giving to not-for-profit organizations as an example, here's how you can use the SMART acronym to go after that goal as a couple or family:

- Specific: Select and give to *Christian charities*.
- Measurable: Give to *five* Christian charities.

- Achievable: Give to five Christian charities *from 20 percent of our annual income.*
- Relevant: Give to five Christian charities from 20 percent of our annual income *whose causes are most important to us.*
- Time-based: Give to five Christian charities from 20 percent of our annual income whose causes are most important to us *over a two-year period.*

See how one builds upon the next? With each iteration, the goal becomes more defined and doable. It'll take some time to come up with goals this precise, but it's worth the effort, and the conversations you'll have in the process will be challenging and enlightening. Then, with this SMART exercise completed, you can develop a giving plan that allows your behaviors to support that goal. According to Generous Giving,[9] those using a giving plan are more likely to give, and on average allocate approximately 30 percent more to giving than those who do not have a plan.

Once you have specific, measurable goals in place, develop a *process to periodically review* them because priorities can change. Unexpected expenses can arise. Health problems can occur. You want to position yourself to proactively respond to these changes on a regular basis. In addition, a goal, for example, to save $50 each week toward the down payment on a new home should be reviewed weekly to determine your progress. One-year goals should be looked at on a six-month basis, while three to five-year goals can be reviewed annually.

Then, as your goals increase or become more complex, *bring in a trusted, knowledgeable third party* (such as an advisor) who can offer advice and hold you accountable. We worked with a man who was easily distracted. He expressed a clear, measurable, and achievable goal for he and his wife to save $50,000 a year for 10 years so that they could slow down, and he could retire by the time he was 62 years of age. Yet every time we met for a review, they had identified another objective for that money—a new building for their business and a more expensive home—that had little to nothing to do with the original goal. We worked to remind them of their original goal, confirmed that it was still something they wanted to achieve, and then reinforced what they needed to save to achieve it. Yet time and again they came up with new ways to use that money, further delaying them from reaching their goal.

As advisors, our job is to navigate our clients much like a GPS. We determine the most efficient path to their destination and ensure they do not miss an important turn. Sometimes, we must serve as a guardrail, preventing them from driving off a financial cliff by making a poor decision from which they cannot recover. The hardest thing in working with clients is knowing the decisions they're making are counter to their own values and objectives. There are enough things out of your control that can keep you from realizing your goals. The last thing you want to do is get in your own way by making bad decisions.

Having a "why" mindset combined with solid goal-setting will help you grow your money—but you'll still struggle unless you learn to communicate effectively, particularly if you're a couple. Elevating your finances is possible, but only as much as you elevate your communication.

7

Communication:
Elevate Your Relationship

Throughout *The Almighty & the Dollar: A Lifestyle of Generosity*, we've touched on the contrasting ways men and women view money and how they react differently to financial challenges. This points to why good communication with your spouse or accountability partner is absolutely vital when it comes to planning and managing your Live, Give, Owe, Grow pie and fulfilling your goals to enjoy a lifestyle of generosity.

During a financial conference, we attended a dynamic presentation from author and communication expert Shaunti Feldhahn. Using material from her workbook and video kit, *Men, Women, and Money: A Couples' Guide to Navigating Money Better, Together*, she used an airplane analogy to set the stage for her message. When the Wright Brothers mastered flight, she said, it was because they figured out that an aircraft needs a rudder in order to stay in the air. You can have the engine and you can achieve lift, but without the rudder, the airplane will not stay in the air. Communication is the rudder that elevates a relationship and keeps it from crashing.

With that in mind, Feldhahn then shared findings from an ongoing study of how men and women communicate with each other—and it was eye-opening.

First, she said their interactions are not about money itself as much as it is about how money makes them *feel*. She used the example of a woman who wanted her husband to pick up Chinese food for dinner versus eating the chicken that was already in the refrigerator. To the wife, getting takeout would give her more time with him and their children after working all day, but the husband saw cooking the chicken for everyone as an affirmation that he was the provider. However, she took his choice as undermining the emotional value she felt about the time they'd spend with one another. The husband wasn't aware of the emotion driving her decision and, therefore, upset her when he didn't intend to. Feldhahn says the same dynamic often comes into play in discussions about money.

> Communication is the rudder that elevates a relationship and keeps it from crashing.

In addition, she talked about how men and women have different *insecurities* and that both tend to use money as an antidote for those feelings. The majority of women, she said, want to know they are special, beautiful, and worthy, while most men want to know they are respected and needed. In relation to money, over 75 percent of these same men desire financial security, but an almost equal percentage of those women are willing to forfeit that financial security as long as they feel loved.

Feldhahn pointed out how men and women *process* decisions differently. Women are much more willing to spend money to close an open window; in other words, to solve a problem. She likened this to the windows you'd find on a computer desktop. Women will have ten windows open at once, and if money can close one of them so she can focus on the others, she will do that. Men, meanwhile, have one window open at a time. They finish that, close it, and then go to the next one. We see this trend all the time as financial advisors. Women are very willing to write a check and be done with it, whether it is to pay off a debt or support a child, because she sees money as the tool to fix the problem.

Feldhahn also shared how their study compared and contrasted couples who had *margin,* meaning they have a regular surplus of money, versus those who did not have margin and are scraping by paycheck to paycheck. What they found was those who have a margin but don't communicate well are actually under more stress in their relationship than couples that don't have a margin and do communicate. In other words, people who have more money but no communication end up with anxiety and disagreements because they have to make more financial decisions. If a couple is young, newly married, and there's no money left after paying the bills, what is there to fight about? They don't feel the weight of those decisions. It's once they gain more of a margin that they begin to experience increased friction.

In the end, you can actually have more money, but have less joy and be under more stress. That's exactly the opposite of the "if you just have a little more, you'll be happy" message our culture proclaims.

Financial speaking among couples

Another insight from Feldhahn was that half of all couples actually don't enjoy talking about finances at all. Therefore, a financial advisor's part as a *facilitator* of discussions about money is essential. Often, we see our role as getting them both in the same room where they know the sole topic is going to be finances: not just account balances, but the purpose of money. What are their goals and objectives? We then ask questions of each one to pull out what is important to them about money and why. Many times, generosity is a pleasant and invigorating way to start this conversation with couples, and it can lead more easily to deeper discussions about retirement, investing, and even what would happen if one of them was gone.

Ecclesiastes 4:9 teaches, "Two people are better off than one, for they can help each other succeed," Therefore, we also try to give each person an equal voice, especially when dealing with struggles they are having about money. The tendency is for the spouse who makes the financial decisions to drive the discussion, but we want to draw out how the other person thinks and feels as well. All too often, we've seen what should be a trialogue between the couple and the advisor turn into a dialogue where the non-decision-making spouse is left out of the discussion. It is important to give the quieter spouse the chance to ask questions that might not get addressed otherwise.

In one session, we had a husband who was kind but very technically-minded. He loved conversations about account balances and rates of return. The wife, though, simply wanted to know whether or not it was a good idea to co-sign on a mortgage with their daughter. It was a philosophical, big picture sort of question. He didn't actually roll his eyes, but his body language certainly seemed to wonder, "Why are we talking about this?" We ended up having a great conversation, but if she hadn't been given an opportunity to ask that question, it might have been something that later became a point of division between them. As a couple, remember that each of your opinions is important, so make sure both of you have a chance to speak and are heard. This is done by asking open-ended questions. "What do you think?" "What questions do you have?" Then be quiet and listen.

When communicating about money, understanding our different *listening styles* as men and women is key. Men tend to dream out loud, Feldhahn said, by sharing with their wives about something they are contemplating but may not actually end up doing. Connie used to tell their kids that John was "just talking to think" when he did that. Their wives will sometimes say or do something to put a stop to that "dream speak" right away, causing the husband to shut down. Similarly, women process issues by talking aloud to their husbands. Men often don't give their wives enough time to express her thoughts before trying to solve the problem in their minds. Instead, husbands need to hear their wives out, and then be given time to process everything before coming back with ideas that the couple can discuss further to arrive at a solution together. It's easy to see how either one of these tendencies can negatively affect communication about dreams or issues regarding money.

Often, communication problems about money don't rise to the surface until a crisis occurs. Everything's fine when the income is good and the retirement plan is on track, but when something like a job loss or major health problem happens, finances can go from being a non-existent issue to the most important problem a couple is facing.

We had one couple where the husband lost his job and then suddenly became ill. The wife told us, "I don't know what is going on. I don't feel financially secure. We are not just talking about money. It's much more than that." She didn't care about markets or investment portfolios. Rather, she wanted to know how to make sure she was going to be okay and keep her family in their existing home. That's why we strive to create dialogue between the husband and wife before there is a crisis. That way, both of them are that much more prepared when difficulty comes.

Then there are those times when deeper issues emerge that are escalated by poor communication. In another case, the husband was an engineer who was smart and loved his career but didn't communicate well with his wife. During the session, she began yelling at him because she didn't know when he was going to retire and what things were going to look like for them afterward. When asked about that, he didn't want to even discuss it. He saw meaning in his work and value in his ability to provide through it. She wanted him to be home to spend time with the family and do some of the things she wanted them to do together. Clearly, this had been simmering under the surface and it exploded in the meeting.

Money talk takeaways

Communication, Feldhahn said, can either create connection or conflict—and we've seen it do both when money is concerned. Ultimately, she concluded that thriving couples are those who have the ability to talk as a team about their finances. Here are some tips you can take away to make that reality for you.

> Communication, can either create connection or conflict—and we've seen it do both when money is concerned.

1. Decide that you are committed to doing this *together*. Accomplishing any goals, particularly financial ones, requires effort and dedication from both husband and wife. If one person isn't on board, they can work counter to the goals and create problems. There was an occasion with one of our clients where the husband found out the wife had accumulated almost $40,000 in credit card debt. While he understood they were trying to save everything they could for retirement, she was doing her own thing. You can't take one step forward if your spouse is taking two steps back. When both partners are committed to shared goals, it is less likely either person will do anything to undermine them.

2. Set *big picture* goals. Starting with your values and using the goal-setting insight we shared to close out the previous chapter, establish your goals as a team, write them down, and have

regular interaction about them. Review and revise the goals at least once a year. This allows you to make sure you are on the same page and are striving for the same objectives. Consider including your family in the conversation, even your children when you feel they are old enough to understand and contribute.

3. Leave room for *brainstorming*. For women, that means talking it out. For men, that means to step away and think, then come back to discuss. Consider scheduling "money dates" once or twice a year, apart from the goal reviews, to discuss where you stand financially as a household and share ideas. John and Connie often did this on long road trips in the car. They called it "windshield time." However you do it, it's all about prioritizing quality and quantity time together with minimal distraction to discuss your finances.

4. Be prepared to *compromise*. Connie always told John, "Marriage is a 60/40 proposition both ways." In general, there is usually one person who is more willing to compromise and the other whose stronger personality makes them less liable to meet halfway. Be aware of the tendencies in your relationship and seek that happy medium where give and take is accepted.

5. Be *transparent* with one another. Ask yourself, "Is there is a barrier to me being able to share everything about my spending with my spouse?" If there is, admit to it. Financial success is unlikely unless you are transparent in your marriage, and a lack of transparency in your finances may be a symptom of greater issues of mistrust and irresponsibility. If you desire, you can have separate accounts, but there should be nothing to hide.

6. Engage *support* when needed. Proverbs 15:22 declares, "Plans go wrong for lack of advice; many advisers bring success." Seek the advice of an advisor who can help you as the money conversation becomes harder and the decisions become more complex. You can be plugging along just fine, but then get more margin and find you are not ready to make all of the decisions by yourselves. If you are single or widowed, your advisor can interact with you regarding your finances.

7. *Celebrate* when you have financial success. Do something enjoyable when you reach milestones and make this an ongoing process. In other words, let's say your goal is to increase your giving from two percent of your income to 10 percent. Don't wait until the end to party! Celebrate when you reach five percent. Or twice, when you hit four percent and seven percent. This brings even more joy to your generosity!

Living the Lifestyle

Properly handling your finances and developing a lifestyle of generous giving is less about numbers and tax law and more about emotion and relationships. We spend more time educating our clients, as we have in *The Almighty & the Dollar: A Lifestyle of Generosity*, than doing statistics or quantitative analysis. The numbers and the technical aspect do matter, but what typically makes people successful is the relational, behavioral aspect of money management: goal setting, communication, and the correct allocation of resources in your Live, Give, Owe, and Grow pie so that you can experience joy with your finances.

This doesn't have to be daunting or overwhelming. It's simply about being intentional and understanding what you are trying to accomplish based on your values. It's also about understanding the difference between rules and principles. You can only put so much money in an IRA. That is a rule. The principle behind investing in an IRA is delayed gratification. You don't know what you will need down the line, so you make a decision now to invest that'll help make sure you have what you need in the future.

In the end, we've discovered that being generous and seeking contentment is more gratifying than having more or making the perfect decision every time. We believe the families we serve who are content because of their generosity have the greatest joy about their money because they live by a simple formula: give first, save second, and spend last.

This lifestyle could not only bring you financial independence, but it positions you to actively follow through on your giving.

Suddenly, it's not all about saving for your own future or accumulating more for today. It's about what you can give back and do with your money to better the world around you, putting others before yourself. It's a truly great way to live!

How do you begin? It starts with asking yourself three vital questions:

1. "Who are the people most important to me?"
2. "What are the causes I care about most?"
3. "How is the use of my money impacting those people and causes?"

A look at your bank statement will quickly reveal the answer to the last question, and will also let you know how your spending, saving, and giving are aligned—or out of whack—with your values and what you want to achieve in life.

Then, when you have your answers, come together with your spouse and/or a financial professional and create your Live, Give, Owe, Grow pie. You'll work to fulfill the exhortation from Proverbs 3:9-10 that says, "Honor the Lord with your wealth and with the best part of everything you produce. Then he will fill your barns with grain, and your vats will overflow with good wine."

Don't hesitate. Your lifestyle of generosity awaits!

Notes

1 Felix Salmon, "By the numbers: Americans are barely in control of their money," www.axios.com

2 Generous Community Initiative, "Understanding and Encouraging Generosity," Albuquerque Edition, Tijeras Foundation.

3 Jill Foley Turner, "This is your brain on generosity," https://www.ncfgiving.com/stories/this-is-your-brain-on-generosity/?utm_campaign=saturday7&utm_source=mailchimp&utm_medium=email&utm_content=01_this_is_your_brain_on_generosity

4 "'Tis the Season for Giving: New Survey Reveals Gifting Experiences On the Rise," https://www.eventbrite.com/blog/press/press-releases/tis-season-giving-new-survey-reveals-gifting-experiences-rise/

5 Video, "Madame Blueberry: A lesson in…Thankfulness," www.youtube.com/watch?v=eR4ymou4D8o, and Transcript, www.veggietalesitsforthekids.wikia.com/wiki/Madame_Blueberry_(episode;_transcript)

6 Transcript, "The Facebook Dilemma: A Two-Night Special Event," www.pbs.org/wgbh/frontline/film/facebook-dilemma/transcript/

7 Article by Karen Demasters, December 4, 2018, "Nearly 40% Of Retirees Overspend, Survey Says," www.fa-mag.com/news/many-retirees-overspend-42184.html

8 Luke 14:28

9 www.generousgiving.org